Aberdeen
Football Club

1. Joe O' Neil is too quick for these Stirling Albion defenders as he slips the fourth goal in a 5-0 rout on 11 September 1954. The previous season at Pittodrie, the Dons had thrashed Stirling Albion 8-0 (Paddy Buckley scoring a hat-trick). If Albion ever entertained hopes of exacting revenge during the 1955-56 season they were to be sorely disappointed - this time they were trounced 7-0! (Johnny Allan scoring four of the seven).

Alastair Guthrie

First published in 1988 by

Archive Publications Ltd
Carrington Business Park
Urmston
Manchester

in association with

The Evening Express
Lang Stracht
Mastrick
Aberdeen

Designed by Clive Hardy: Cover by Lorraine Shaw

Production by Richardson Press

ISBN 0 948946 23 7

2. Hearts defenders are relieved to watch Paddy Buckley miss this chance by inches as the Dons pushed for the Championship. Aberdeen still took both points from this one through a Harry Yorston strike.

Contents

Foreword
by
Dick Donald

It has often been said that one picture tells a thousand words, so what better way to present a history of Aberdeen FC than through a series of fine photographs, tracing the club back to its inception?

Throughout the years Aberdeen FC have never been lacking in initiative, with developments which have not only benefitted the club, but also Scottish football in general.

We were pleased when it was recognised that Pittodrie Stadium was the first all-seated, all-covered football ground in Britain and also when the club had a voice in negotiations leading to the formation and shape of the Premier League.

Now we have given our backing to this official pictorial history of Aberdeen FC. Once again, it is the first of its kind involving a Scottish side.

Our supporters will be able to enjoy once more our Cup and Championship triumphs over the years, though the disappointments of defeat have also been recorded.

That rainy night in Gothenburg when the club became holders of the European Cup-Winners' Cup will never be forgotten by those who were there with us in the Ullevi Stadium or by the thousands more who watched the tie on television back home.

It was a remarkable performance by our players and supporters, who have been a credit throughout Europe.

Older fans, however, will also recall with great joy the seasons when the Scottish Cup and the Championship came to Pittodrie for the first time. Those of more tender years have savoured our recent victories.

I'm sure the fans will agree that since the club's first game in 1903 we have attracted some of the finest players and managers to Pittodrie. It is our intention to see that future seasons are as successful and memorable as those years which have slipped by.

Dick Donald.
Chairman

Introduction

Dick Donald's links with the Dons stretch back to 1928 when he signed on as a wing half from juvenile club St. Nicholas. Little did Aberdeen know that decades later his guidance and knowledge would steer the club through the most successful period in their history.

It wasn't until August 1949 that Richard Macnaughton Donald was invited to join the board of directors. And when the Dons opened season 1970-71 as Scottish Cup holders they did so with a new chairman, Dick Donald, one of the city's most prominent and successful businessmen. Charles Forbes resigned after twelve years in the chair to make way for the younger director, who had been vice-chairman for ten years.

The new man at the helm made this pledge: "It is my hope that the winning of the Scottish Cup will herald the start of a successful era for the Dons. Every effort will be made to keep the club in the forefront of Scottish football". But even an optimistic new chairman could not have envisaged that Aberdeen would go on to clean sweep the domestic scene and conquer Europe under his astute leadership.

The reorganisation was completed by the appointment of Chris Anderson, who had served on the board for three years, as vice-chairman. Aberdeen were not only on a granite-solid footing, but they also had men of unquestionable character and vision at the forefront. It was an inspired pairing which would transform the club on the field and propel Pittodrie years ahead of the pack as Britain's first all-seated, all-covered stadium. Although the achievements were plentiful, the full potential was probably never fully realised. For in May 1986 Scottish football was left to mourn the passing of Chris Anderson after his year-long fight against motor neurone disease. Chris Anderson, awarded the OBE in 1981 for his services to Scottish sport, was a man who had always looked to the future and was the principal architect behind the Premier League.

Aberdeen have the tradition of being known as a family club and Dick Donald's son, Ian, was named as a director in 1980. Ian, another former senior player whose clubs had included Manchester United, has since taken over the vice-chairman's role. The Dons had seven directors when Dick Donald moved on to the board in 1949 but his policy was to run a tight ship with a minimum of captains. As a result Aberdeen completed their eighty-fifth year with only three directors, one of whom was bookmaker Bobby Morrison who had been invited on board in 1987.

3. The Dons at Aberdeen Station in 1969. *back row:* coach Jimmy Bonthrone, George Murray, Chic McLelland, Jim Hermiston, Henning Boel, Ernie McGarr, Jens Petersen, Tommy McMillan, Jim Forrest. *crouching:* Tommy Wilson, Jim Hamilton, Alex Willoughby, Dave Robb, Tommy Rae.

Gothenburg Glory 1983

The rain came cascading down to give the Red Army a real Swedish soaking. But no-one cared. The 12,000 strong red and white legion, who had travelled to the sprawling sea port of Gothenburg by anything from chartered flight to fishing boat, had just witnessed their team realise an impossible dream - winning in Europe.

Real Madrid, those arrogant aristocrats, had fallen by 2-1 to the homespun Dons. Aberdeen were the proud new holders of the Cup-Winners' Cup and tears of joy could not be distinguished from rain drops as the celebrations ignited in the Ullevi Stadium.

It had been a long, hard campaign through a preliminary round in Switzerland and on to the competition proper in Albania, Poland, West Germany and Belgium. Aberdeen earned the right to face the Spaniards by swamping Sion with eleven goals; squeezing Dinamo Tirana into submission; defeating Lech Poznan twice; bewildering Bayern Munich; and walking over Waterschei.

And the Dons were not to be denied their finest hour in Gothenburg. Real had displayed a near contempt for their final opponents. But those same Spanish players and officials were to disappear "like sna' aff a dyke" (as one Don said) when Willie Miller accepted the European prize out there on a sodden pitch.

Aberdeen made the start they wanted . . . and Real feared as Eric Black flashed an early volley inches over Augustin's bar. Better was to follow when Black scored. But the Cup was far from being in Aberdeen's comfortable care as the men from the Bernabeu made it all square through a Juanito penalty at full time.

But supersub John Hewitt, who had replaced a limping Black, chose the right moment in extra time to amble unguarded into the penalty box to despatch a close-in header from a Mark McGhee cross past the outstretched Augustin. The glory belonged to Aberdeen.

4. Ecstasy for Aberdeen's European prize guys. Taking up the rear on the Ullevi pitch are Neale Cooper, Alex McLeish, John Hewitt, Peter Weir, Mark McGhee, Ian Angus, Eric Black, Jim Leighton, Gordon Strachan, Bryan Gunn, Andy Watson. Crouching with the Cup are John McMaster, Stuart Kennedy, Doug Rougvie, Willie Miller, Neil Simpson.

5. The Flying Dons prepare to jet out for Gothenburg and a date with destiny.

6. The Dons acknowledge their huge support. *from the left:* Bryan Gunn, Andy Watson, Ian Angus, John Hewitt, Stuart Kennedy, Alex McLeish, Neale Cooper, Doug Rougvie, Neil Simpson, Eric Black, Peter Weir, Gordon Strachan, Mark McGhee, John McMaster, Jim Leighton, Willie Miller.

7. The shape of things to come. An Eric Black volley is fingertipped on to the bar by Real keeper Augustin only three minutes into the final.

8. But there was no denying Eric Black in the sixth minute when he hooked the ball home after Alex McLeish had headed down a corner.

9. There were even torrid times when Archie Knox couldn't bear to look.

10. Tension on the bench is unbearable as Alex Ferguson, Archie Knox and the subs kick every ball.

11. Tempers and temperaments were stretched to the limit as the Dons and Real Madrid's Manager Alfredo Di Stefano (*left*) urged their men for one final push.

12. The goal dreams are made of. Super sub John Hewitt heads in the winner past a despairing Augustin in the 111th minute.

13. Hewitt's reel set the nation dancing with delight as the ball lies tucked at the back of the Real net.

14. There's no tension now, just pure joy as Alex Ferguson and Archie Knox take a deserved lap of honour.

15. Look what I've got, lads. Goal hero John Hewitt takes a throw-in with the European prize.

16. Rougvie and captain Miller stride forward to thank the drenched Red Army for their vocal efforts.

17. Riding high. Alex Ferguson gets a lift from Peter Weir and Doug Rougvie.

18. The fans who couldn't make it to Sweden celebrate.

19. The striking young pair hold aloft the Cup-Winners' Cup.

20. Alex Ferguson and Mark McGhee had the Cup at the quayside to welcome back the fans who had made the voyage over the North Sea on the *St. Clair*.

21. The biggest street party ever seen in Aberdeen was sparked off by the Dons' European triumph.

22. Only a few days later the banner on the bus was amended to include another Scottish Cup victory at the end of an unforgettable season.

THE DON'S ARE THE GREATEST. WINNERS OF EUROPEAN CUP WINNERS CUP 1983 ALSO SCOTTISH CUP WINNERS 1983

Northern SCOTTISH

23. The SFA commemorated Aberdeen's Gothenburg glory when president Tommy Younger presented these decanters to chairman Dick Donald. *from the left:* director Ian Donald, chairman Donald, manager Alex Ferguson, President Younger, SFA secretary Ernie Walker, vice-chairman Chris Anderson.

24. Manager Alex Ferguson and his players put the Aberdeenshire Cup, European Cup-Winners' Cup and Scottish Cup on show.

I. Vice-chairman Ian Donald, chairman Dick Donald and director Bobby Morrison admire the solid silver model of the Bernabeu Stadium, presented by Real Madrid to mark the 1983 Cup-Winners' final.

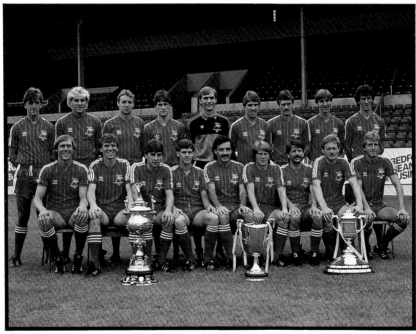

II. Sandwiched between the Aberdeenshire Cup and the Scottish Cup lies Aberdeen's biggest prize, the Cup-Winners' Cup. *back row:* Weir, Cooper, Cowan, Angus, Leighton, McGhee, Bell, Mitchell, Stark. *front:* Rougvie, McLeish, Hewitt, Black, Miller, Strachan, Kennedy, McMaster, Simpson.

III. Ian Porterfield, manager of the Dons from November 1986 until his resignation in May 1988.

IV. The Super Cup, which isn't a Cup at all, but a splendid plaque, has pride of place in the Pittodrie boardroom.

V. New technology has taken over behind the scenes at Pittodrie. Secretary Ian Taggart and the computer definitely know which side to support.

Lean and Hungry 1903-1937

Willie McAulay is not a name which features automatically on any list of Aberdeen greats. Yet the inside left holds two records which can never be broken. When the Aberdeen FC that the fans love and follow today made their Pittodrie debut on 15 August 1903, manager Jimmy Philip asked Willie McAulay to lead the fledgling club into action against Stenhousemuir. Interest in this new venture was high and 8000 were inside the ground when Aberdeen's first captain scored their first goal in a 1-1 draw.

Aberdeen were on their way...just four months after three prominent city clubs - Orion, Victoria United and Aberdeen - agreed it was time to gell their resources. Amalgamation had been talked about, generally in whispers, since football was first played in the North-East. On 14 April 1903, it became a reality.

The three united clubs took other equally important decisions. Qualified referee Philip, a native Aberdonian, was to occupy the first managerial chair, with former Victoria United trainer Peter Simpson at his side.

resumed his full-time job with the club. But four years later and with several more feuds with the authorities behind him, Philip resigned to make way for Pat Travers. Just before he moved out, however, Philip produced a master signing stroke in bringing Alex Jackson - a Wembley Wizard of the future - to Pittodrie.

A former Aberdeen player, the much-travelled Travers used his far-reaching overseas network to strengthen a reshaped team. Midway through his rule he had already moulded genuine championship contenders. Despite surging through season 1929-30 unbeaten at home - the only club in Britain to achieve this honour - the title itself eluded the Dons. Travers and his coach Donald Colman were burning for a break. And if it had not been for Colman's quick act as a fireman in 1931, Pittodrie could have gone up in smoke. A blaze had been fuelled by a jersey falling on a fire in a stand drying room. Colman prevented the potential disaster.

The pair did, however, snap the Dons out of a Scottish Cup semi final jinx. After many brave but unproductive attempts Aberdeen at last booked a place alongside Celtic before an all time record 146,433 Hampden crowd on 24 April 1937. The Scottish Cup, however, was destined not to make its first journey north.

Matt Armstrong cancelled out Johnny Crum's opener, but a controversial Willie Buchan goal gave the Celts the silver. Pat Travers, with a taste for the exotic, had journeyed his Dons to South Africa in 1927 and he returned ten years later before accepting a job with Clyde in November of that year, which left a lean Aberdeen still hungry for that first trophy... and looking to appoint a third manager.

Pittodrie, which had already been altered quite a bit since the time when it was employed by the police as a dung hill for their horses, was to be home. And the new club were to retain the white shirts worn by the original Aberdeen. But Aberdeen failed in a bid to be balloted into the First Division and an oversight kept them out of the Second Division. So it had to be Northern League football and Aberdeen had to bide their time before moving up into the senior circles.

Within two seasons Aberdeen had enhanced the Second Division and had been voted into the top League, where their white jerseys had given way to resplendent new black and gold colours. The Whites had become the Wasps. Today's accepted and accustomed nickname, the Dons - probably a shortening of Aberdonian - didn't ring around the terracing until 1913.

Philip, who was a shrewd organiser and a bit of an extrovert, gained credibility for the club by taking them into a Scottish Cup semi final in 1908 - the same year that winger Willie Lennie became Aberdeen's first Scotland player. Three years later they achieved a runners-up berth behind Rangers in the First Division.

The bowler-hatted, moustachioed Philip had a liking for the extraordinary and he even arranged an unprecedented tour of Bohemia and Moravia for Aberdeen during years when even an outing to the beach at Balmedie was viewed as a major event. Despite being a member of several official committees, Philip was generally a man at war with the authorities - some things never seem to change for managers.

The First World War caused football to take a secondary seat and it wasn't until 1920 that Philip

25. Jimmy Phillip, Aberdeen's first manager and later a director. A road accident in Belfast in July 1930 led to his death three months later.

26. It's April 1882 and the first AFC are on parade. But only one player sported the distinctive, embroidered club badge on his jersey.

27. The gentlemen of the Press at the rear of the photograph were well covered as Aberdeen and Victoria United posed for the camera before the Charity Cup final in May 1895.

28. Shin guards have developed considerably since the "armoured plating" worn by this Aberdeen team of 1899. And how about those studless boots and extra strong belts for the heavy-duty breeches!

29. The impressive Aberdeenshire Cup takes pride of place for the Whites in 1902.

30. Nets for the goals hadn't even been considered at Cattofield when Orion faced Victoria United prior to the 1903 amalgamation.

31. Only a season before the amalgamation the Aberdeen Football Team held this photo-call at the Chanonry in Old Aberdeen.

32. Management and players from 1907-8.

33. Three fans crept into this group alongside chairman Thomas Duncan (*back right*). Most of the Black and Gold players here took part in Aberdeen's first ever Scottish Cup semi final in March 1908. A 20,000 crowd packed into Pittodrie with great expectations - but Celtic won 1-0.

34. Aberdeen keepers were trend-setters in season 1912-13 with these stylish jerseys. *top row, left to right:* F. Watson, A. King, A. Greig, Wm. Milne, Wm. Low. *second row:* R. Hannah, A. Gault, D. Main, J. Hume, G. Wilson, J. Walker, J. McConnell. *third row:* S. Davidson, J. Edgar, P. Travers, W. Lennie, D. Colman, J. Soye, J. Wood, C. Nelson, W. Brown.

36. Pittodrie is the backdrop for this early benefit. Peter Simpson is holding a tray of watches which he later presented to the Aberdeen and Morton players.

37. Charles Forbes, later to rise through the ranks to become club chairman, is seated on the right of the second row.

35. Donald Colman, seen here in 1911 four years after joining Aberdeen, was probably Aberdeen's first real hero. But his surname was not Colman at all, but Cunningham. He adopted his granny's surname to register as a junior to keep his beloved football activities secret from a stern, disapproving father.

The legendary Colman, a right-back with the emphasis on brain not brawn, became the oldest Don to win a first cap at the age of thirty-three. In fact, he was still playing for Aberdeen at forty-two. He scored only one goal for the club - in a 4-2 home defeat by Queens Park in September 1916 - but prevented countless more.

In 1942 at the age of sixty-four Donald Colman died of tuberculosis. Colman left an everlasting mark on the game as during his spell as club trainer in the 1930s his innovation brought the trainer's dug-out to Pittodrie - the first of its kind in Britain.

38. Manager Pat Travers is on the right of this team group from 1926-27.

39. Two versions of the old black and gold strips as Aberdeen embark for South Africa in 1927.

ABERDEEN FOOTBALL CLUB 1928-29

MERRIE, COOPER, DONALD, McHALE, McLAREN, McKENZIE, LEGGE,

RITCHIE, (Asst. Trainer) BLACK, SMITH, JACKSON, BLACKWELL, YUILL, LOVE, McLEOD, LIVINGSTONE, RUSSELL, (Trainer)

ROBERTSON, (Secretary) POLLAND, WILSON, FALLOON, McDERMID, (CAPTAIN), MUIR, YORSTON, CHEYNE, HILL, TRAVERS, (MANAGER)

TROPHIES. FLEMING SHIELD - ABERDEENSHIRE COUNTY CUP - ABERDEEN DISTRICT LEAGUE CUP - DEWAR CHALLENGE SHIELD.

40. Trophies on show in 1928-9. The Fleming Shield, Aberdeenshire Cup, Aberdeen District League Cup and the Dewar Shield are on display. Benny Yorston (*front row, fourth from right*), scored 125 goals between 1927 and 1932 and set up a club League record of 28 goals in season 1929-30.

41. A souvenir from 1932-33.

42. Bunnets were a necessity as this cloth-capped brigade head down Merkland Road East in 1937 for a game against Celtic.

43. A section of the 30,000 crowd which flocked to Pittodrie to watch a 1-1 draw with Rangers on 20 March 1937.

SOUTH ENCLOSURE

ENTER ONLY AT TURNSTILES
(See Plan on back)

G

STAND ENTRANCE 1 or 8

Admit to SOUTH ENCLOSURE

Scottish Cup—Final Tie

HAMPDEN PARK, GLASGOW

Saturday, 24th April, 1937

Kick-off 3 p.m.

Price 2/6
(Including Tax)

G. G. Graham
Secretary

THIS PORTION TO BE RETAINED
(See Conditions on back)

No. 735

44. For the princely sum of 2/6 - that's twelve and a half pence today - the fans were treated to a classic final, between Aberdeen and Celtic. It was the Dons first appearance in a Scottish Cup Final and they lost by a single doubtful goal.

45. Matt Armstrong rolls his sleeves up as he steps onto the Hampden turf before a massive 146,433 crowd - an all-time British club record - for the 1937 Scottish Cup final. But not even a flashing Armstrong goal could stop Celtic from winning 2-1.

46. Willie Cooper and Charlie Tully chase a long ball in the Cup final cauldron.

47. And Willie Cooper prepares to bring an end to a promising Celtic raid.

48. The dapper Matt Armstrong was the idol of these Tivoli Tonics chorus girls in the 1930s. Envious eyes are being cast by manager Pat Travers and Irishman Eddie Falloon.

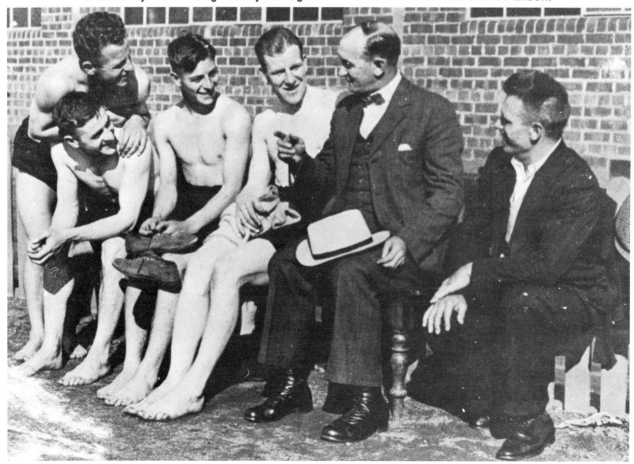

49. A natty white hat lies on the knee of Jock Hume, a full-back from 1907-20. He returned from America in the 1930s to tell these topless Dons a few tales from the "old" days. Matt Armstrong had at least remembered to take his shoes along.

F. & J. SMITH'S CIGARETTES

ABERDEEN.
D. COLMAN.
O.H.M.S.

W. COOPER

VI-X. Donald Colman, Willie Cooper, Matt Armstrong, Willie Mills and Eddie Falloon are the subjects for cigarette cards.

MITCHELL'S CIGARETTES

M. ARMSTRONG
(ABERDEEN)

MITCHELL'S CIGARETTES

W. MILLS
(ABERDEEN)

MITCHELL'S CIGARETTES

E. FALLOON
(ABERDEEN)

M. ARMSTRONG

W. MILLS

XI-XIV. Matt Armstrong, Willie Mills, Eddie Falloon and South African born Billy Strauss as portrayed by *Bos* for the *Well Known Footballer* series of cards issued by John Sinclair Ltd.

E. FALLOON

W. STRAUSS

50. All ship-shape in May 1937. The Dons are on board the *Stirling Castle* bound for South Africa. Vice-chairman William Mitchell, later to become chairman, is on the right of the front row.

51. This dinner suit momento was taken in Durban. But Aberdeen's sunshine trip turned to tragedy when winger Jackie Benyon was struck by appendicitis and later died in a Johannesburg hospital from peritonitis. *back row:* Willie Cooper, Billy Scott, Herbert Currer, Bob Temple, Billy Strauss. *middle row:* Jackie Benyon, Johnny McKenzie, Frank Dunlop, George Thomson, Eddie Falloon, Johnny Lang. *front row:* Captain Bobby Fraser, South African team manager S. V. Kimber, Chairman Frank Whitehead, Manager Pat Travers, Trainer Donald Colman.

52. Willie Mills, who had been pitched straight into the team as a tender seventeen year old in 1932, catches up on the Dons' progress in the Green Final.

53. Matt Armstrong was awarded this Scottish junior cap for a game against Ireland in 1930.

54. Terrible twins from yesteryear Matt Armstrong and Willie Mills return to Pittodrie to relive some great goals.

Taste of Success 1938-1965

When the bells peeled in 1938, Aberdeen stepped into the New Year with a new manager, Dave Halliday. There had been no shortage of contenders for the vacant post and over a hundred men, good and true, supplied Pittodrie with applications. The choice of Halliday surprised many Dons followers. Like Travers and Philip before him, the former Dundee, Sunderland, Arsenal and Manchester City goal scorer did not become directly involved in training, preferring to leave the physical sweat and toil to his right hand men.

But unlike previous managers he brought eagerly-awaited success to the Dons in the shape of the country's major prizes, the Scottish Cup and the Championship. Before Halliday's seventeen years were over, Aberdeen were to have their name engraved in Scottish football's book of fame as winners.

The early years for Halliday were hard and the most significant change took place in 1939 when the black and gold stripes gave way to today's traditional red.

The Second World War cancelled official League football and directors Charles Forbes and George Anderson ran the side while Halliday, players and fans did their bit for King and country. In fact,

Pittodrie was designated an Air Raid Precautions post! The wartime Dons were a mixture of special guests and Pittodrie soldiers. A rising star called Stan Mortensen had been persuaded to go to Aberdeen to feature alongside the likes of Matt Armstrong and Jack Pattillo.

The Mitchell Trophy, donated by Aberdeen chairman William Mitchell, frequently remained at Pittodrie. But the national breakthrough was achieved on 11 May 1946, when, before a huge 135,000 crowd at Hampden, Aberdeen defeated Rangers by 3-2 to claim the Southern League Cup. The classic final, the first in Scotland for seven war-torn years, has since been regarded as the first real League Cup final. Aberdeen, two up through Archie Baird and Stan Williams, appeared to be coasting to victory . . . until Rangers made it dramatically all square at 2-2. The tide seemed to have turned against the Dons as amateur winger Alec Kiddie and Andy Cowie struck wood. But George Taylor's last-gasp goal brought that first silver to Aberdeen.

The Trophy was to stay in Aberdeen's safe care for only a matter of weeks, as a twist of fate and circumstance had it quickly renamed the Victory Cup. It remains at Ibrox to this very day, having

55. Forfar Athletic's James Black presents the Mitchell Cup to Frank Dunlop after a 7-3 aggregate win over Raith Rovers in May 1943.

been handed over to the Southern League Cup losers Rangers.

The Dons obviously enjoyed Hampden's unique Cup final flavour as they were back in position twice in the following year. Aberdeen gained the distinction of being the first club to make it into both the League Cup and the Scottish Cup finals in the same season.

There were to be no double celebrations as Rangers gained sweet revenge in the League Cup with a runaway 4-0 trouncing on a windswept April afternoon. Two weeks later, on 19 April, it was to be a tale of triumph for captain Frank Dunlop.

The Dons were unsettled when the reliable Willie Cooper had to miss the match through injury and worse was to follow when Hibs snatched an early lead. But a more composed Aberdeen coped with the difficult situation. Goals from Gentleman George Hamilton and Stan Williams ensured that the Scottish Cup was paraded through city streets for the first time. Cooper, injured in the semi final, was invited to take part in the Hampden party before 82,140 fans.

Halliday had his Dons back at Hampden in quick succession to face the Old Firm. But twice the Scottish Cup stayed west, in 1953 and 1954. Harry Yorston breathed hope into a flagging Aberdeen with an equaliser ten minutes from time against Rangers, but the Light Blues took the replay by 1-0. Then Celtic had a slender 2-1 win the following year after Aberdeen had annihilated Rangers 6-0 in the semi finals, recording their first success over the Ibrox giants in this competition.

The most glittering domestic prize of all, the Championship, was delivered to Pittodrie by Halliday in season 1954-55. It was a moment to be cherished as the title crown was not scheduled to return for another twenty-five long years. An Archie Glen penalty against Clyde at Shawfield on 9 April 1955, confirmed that the Dons were the best

in the A Division; but when the Championship Trophy moved in, the successful Halliday moved out to guide Leicester.

No-one could have envied Dave Shaw, the former club captain who was logically promoted from trainer to manager. But within months it was celebration time again as the side Shaw had groomed and Halliday had shaped lifted the League Cup. St. Mirren fell by 2-1 on 22 October 1955, when Graham Leggat added to the Saints' misery of an own goal.

Standards and the flow of silver could not be maintained. Injuries to key players didn't help Shaw's task and it was discovered that Lady Luck had a forked tongue. Striker Harry Yorston won a fortune on the Pools and immediately announced a premature retirement at the age of only twenty-eight.

An appearance in the 1959 Scottish Cup final helped to take the fans' minds off the barren years and the struggles to avoid the indignity of relegation. But a 3-1 defeat by St. Mirren helped to hurry the inevitable along - Shaw resumed his duties as club trainer and handed over the manager's reins to former team-mate Tommy Pearson in November 1959.

Even the newly-installed floodlighting system couldn't make the Dons shine. The ever-polite Pearson was fraught with relegation worries and unacceptable Scottish Cup results, including humiliating defeats from lowly Ayr United and East Fife. Indeed, that dreadful Cup demise at Bayview on 10 February 1965, which came directly on top of an 8-0 Parkhead pounding, led directly to Pearson's resignation.

The Dons directors refused to rush and more than two weeks passed before they invited the Queen's Park coach to Pittodrie for talks. His name was Eddie Turnbull.

56. Breakthrough. The Southern League Cup becomes Aberdeen property in May 1946. Dons from the left are: Taylor, Cowie, Johnstone, Baird, Dunlop, McKennie, Hamilton, Kiddie.

57. It's standing room only outside Aberdeen Joint Station as the fans wait for the Dons and the 1946 Southern League Cup.

58. Aberdeen's first major capture, the 1945-46 Southern League Cup, is proudly shown off after a 3-2 triumph over Rangers. *back row:* Bob McDermid (trainer), Andy Cowie, Willie Cooper, George Johnstone, Pat McKenna, George Taylor, Dave Halliday (manager). *front row:* Alex Kiddie, George Hamilton, Stan Williams, Frank Dunlop, Archie Baird, Billy McCall.

59 & 60. *above left:* An autographed ball bearing the legend "Signatures of the Mighty" goes on show along with a picture of the Winning Goal - and the Southern League Cup itself - in the *Evening Express* window. *above right:* The pride of the north in 1947. *back row:* McLaughlin, Cooper, McKenna, Johnstone, Waddell, Taylor, Dunlop. *front row:* Harris, Hamilton, Williams, Baird, McCall.

61. Referee Bobby Calder, who was later to play a huge part in attracting so many rising stars to Pittodrie as chief scout, watches captains Frank Dunlop and Dave Shaw shake hands before the memorable final.

62. The goal that rekindled Dons hopes and set them on the victory path. Billy McCall raises his arms after George Hamilton's header beat keeper Jimmy Kerr for the equaliser.

63. Victory! South African Stan Williams squeezed the ball home from an impossibly tight angle - and the Cup was on its way to Pittodrie for the first time. Archie Baird (left) was on stand-by.

64. The Scottish Cup is ours. Frank Dunlop finally gets to grips with the trophy.

65. Veteran Willie Cooper gives the Cup a special hug. For a pulled muscle in the 2-0 semi final win over Arbroath only seven days earlier cost Cooper his Hampden place.

66. Jubilant Dons carry captain Frank Dunlop and the Scottish Cup shoulder high. George Taylor, Willie McCall, Pat McKenna, George Hamilton, Joe McLaughlin, Stan Williams, Tony Harris and Willie Waddell join in the celebrations with chairman William Mitchell.

67. Despite a constant downpour thousands of supporters gathered at Aberdeen Joint Station to greet the 1947 Scottish Cup Victors.

68. The winners had to make their way onto the roof of the bus to let their fans see the silver.

69. The Scottish Cup is safe and sound in Aberdeen and still wearing the Dons' victory ribbons.

70. A galloping Frank Dunlop keeps his eye on the ball.

71. Frank Dunlop couldn't resist giving the Scottish Cup a welcome back kiss when the trophy continued to return to Pittodrie in the 1980s.

72. Pittodrie is barely recognisable from this aerial shot in the 1950s from today's super all-seated, all-covered stadium.

73. Fans in the 42,000 gate climbed on advertising hoardings to gain an advantage, while hundreds were locked out of this 1953 Scottish Cup replay against Hibs. Aberdeen won 2-0.

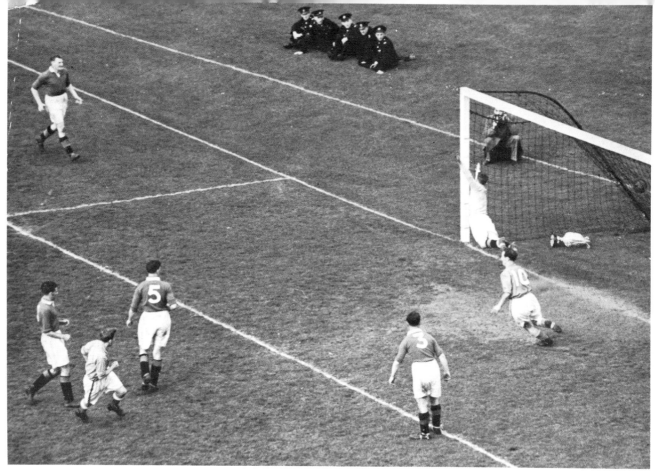

74. Harry Yorston (*second from left*) snatches a late equaliser against Rangers to revive Dons' hopes in the 1953 final.

75. Sheer joy! George Hamilton embraces a delighted Harry Yorston whose goal had just earned Aberdeen a replay in the 1952-53 Scottish Cup.

76. Rangers took the second game 1-0. Many years later the disappointment of the 1953 replay was forgotten as "Gentleman" George Hamilton and Harry Yorston got their hands on the Scottish Cup.

77. Pittodrie was overflowing when Hibs travelled north in 1947 and scores of fans scrambled to a precarious perch on the roof of the stand. But the record attendance was created on 13 March 1954, when a staggering 45,061 watched the Dons beat Hearts 3-0 in the fourth round of the Scottish Cup.

78 & 79. *above left:* Jack Allister, Alec Young and Archie Glen played as smartly as they dressed in 1954 as they marched towards that first title.*above right:* A first for Fred Martin. For the lanky Don was Scotland's keeper when they appeared in the World Cup finals in 1954 for the first time. Fred played in three losing Scottish Cup finals in 1953, 1954 and 1959, but he has the medals from the double trophy-winning side of 1955.

80. Paddy Buckley prods the ball into the Celts net in the 1954 Scottish Cup final, but the trophy was destined to move from Pittodrie to Parkhead.

81. The legendary Jock Stein shields the ball safely back to keeper Bonnar as Jim Clunie (*left*) and Paddy Buckley wait for any slip.

82. Surrounded by the men who brought glory to Pittodrie in season 1954-55, manager Dave Halliday keeps a tight hold of the Championship trophy. Among the familiar faces is Teddy Scott (*second from the right, second row*) the Dons' trainer who hasn't changed much over the years. *back row:* Kelly, Dunbar, Morrison, Martin, Macfarlane. *first row:* Clelland, O'Neil, Clunie, Hay, Scott. *second row:* D. Shaw (trainer), Ingram, Wilson, Glen, W. Smith, I. Smith, John Brown, Wishart, Allister, Wallace, B. Alexander (assistant trainer). *front row:* Allan, Davidson, Jimmy Brown, Paterson, Buckley, manager Halliday, Mitchell, Young, Yorston, Hamilton, Mulhall. Missing are Leggat, Hather and Caldwell.

83. *left:* And it's a sight to be cherished as the mark of Champions flutters over Pittodrie.

84. *above:* Just rewards - a winner's Championship medal from 1955.

85. *below:* The goal that turned a Saint into a Sinner. St Mirren defender Jimmy Mallan can only breast Jackie Hather's cross into his own net as Graham Leggat rushes in during the 1955 League Cup.

XV. Souvenir booklet of photographs, published by the *Evening Express*, to celebrate the outstanding success of Aberdeen in winning the Scottish Cup.

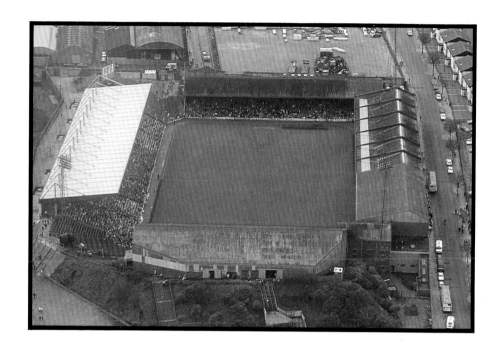

XVI & XVII. Pittodrie Stadium has had many facelifts since
Aberdeen made it their home.

86. Captain Jimmy Mitchell still has his jersey attached to the League Cup. The winners are Graham Leggat, Bobby Wishart, Dave Caldwell, skipper Mitchell, Archie Glen, Harry Yorston, Jim Clunie, Jackie Hather, Fred Martin and chairman Mitchell.

87. Skipper Jimmy Mitchell is swept along at the Joint Station as he brings home the League Cup in 1955.

88. Dave Shaw was aiming high as a player and later as a manager.

89. Bobby Wishart, newly-appointed manager Dave Shaw, Harry Yorston and Hughie Hay peer out from the Pittodrie dug-out.

90 & 91. *above left:* Right-winger Graham Leggat was a Hampden marksman in the 1955 League Cup final win and here he causes all sorts of bother for Airdrie defenders Quigley and Baillie. *above right:* Paddy Buckley could find no way round the bulk of Rangers' centre-half George Young as the Dons were swamped 6-2 before 35,000 in a League Cup qualifying tie at Pittodrie in August 1956.

92. On the ball . . . that was tracksuited Tommy Pearson (recently transferred from Newcastle United) in this 1948 piece of training action. Pearson took over as manager after Dave Shaw stepped down to become coach/trainer in 1959.

93. Chairman Charles Forbes is watched by manager Tommy Pearson as he hands out club scarves as Christmas presents to the players.

94. Tommy Pearson and two unusual souvenirs. The diploma was presented by the FA to mark his appearance as an "emergency" left winger for England in 1939. The cap was for playing for Scotland against England in 1947.

95. Willing hands attempt to scrape the snow and ice off Pittodrie in February 1956. Such a sight is a thing of the past as the Dons now have a £100,000 undersoil heating system.

96. It may have been a grey and misty November 1955, but these Aberdeen and Clyde players still had to take their half-time cuppa on the Pittodrie pitch.

Sweet and Sour 1965-1978

For the next thirteen years the Red Army went through a full range of emotions, from shouting their throats raw in victory, to burying heads in hands in despair as silverware agonisingly slipped through Aberdeen's fingers. Eddie Turnbull, Jimmy Bonthrone, Ally MacLeod and Billy McNeill produced a period of elation and frustration. But the mould for unprecedented success was set by the time McNeill followed MacLeod through Pittodrie's revolving doors after a whistlestop stay.

It was clear from the minute Turnbull placed a first foot inside Pittodrie that he was a strict man, a disciplinarian whose insight into the modern game was unsurpassed at the stadium. Facts speak for themselves, for he handed out no less than seventeen free transfers after only a few months. He knew the level which had to be attained and he would be ruthless in achieving his goal.

Talents such as Bobby Clark, Joe Harper, Martin Buchan and Tommy Craig were to blossom under Turnbull's uncompromising but beneficial management. Success was also to return and, in fact, Turnbull's Tornadoes had a Scottish Cup final

date with Celtic at Hampden by 1967.

This particular fairytale didn't produce a happy-ever-after ending for Aberdeen. Illness caused Turnbull to miss the occasion and the Dons went down by 2-0 to a side who were about to become immortal as the first British winners of the European Cup.

That Hampden final did, however, lead directly to Aberdeen's first appearance in Europe in the Cup-Winners' Cup. Who then would have dared to forecast the glory that lay ahead in the competition?

When the Dons did travel back to Hampden to face Celtic again in 1970, Turnbull was positioned in the dug-out. This time there was an unforgettable conclusion.

Derek McKay, picked up on a free transfer from Dundee, had already been dubbed "Cup tie McKay" after producing the quarter final winner against Falkirk and then supplying a similar deadly finish in the semi finals against Kilmarnock. McKay didn't let the Red Army down at Hampden either as he continued his purple patch with two goals in Aberdeen's storming 3-1 victory over a side once

97. Firemen and club officials survey the extent of the damage after the fire.

more contesting a European Cup final.

Celtic were odds-on favourites against a side who had taken the unusual step in blooding seventeen year old winger Arthur Graham in a Cup final. But the bookies were proved wrong from the moment goals King Joe Harper prodded a cool penalty past Evan Williams.

Martin Buchan became the youngest ever captain to collect the Scottish Cup. Respectability and prestige returned to Pittodrie along with Turnbull and the trophy.

The following season could have brought the Championship itself, but nerves took control on the run-in just as Aberdeen appeared poised to end Celtic's supremacy of many years. Another acute disappointment followed swiftly when Turnbull, a former member of Hibs' exclusive Famous Five, packed his bags for Easter Road.

Aberdeen searched no further afield for a new manager than their backroom - and appointed Jimmy Bonthrone, a pleasant and mannerable man who had been a trusted coach under Turnbull. Bonthrone's placid approach had taken over from Turnbull's brash and abrasive style. The handover resembled a similar change years previously when Halliday gave way to Shaw.

Almost in keeping with Turnbull's firebrand personality, Pittodrie suffered great damage when a blaze destroyed a chunk of the Main Stand in February 1971. Indeed, the Scottish Cup itself had to be rescued from a smoke-filled office through a shattered window by diligent firemen.

Bonthrone won the inaugural Drybrough Cup in 1971 with a victory over Celtic. Strange, because the Dons were also the last winners many years later under Alex Ferguson. Aberdeen had another close Championship shave in 1970-71 when they again completed the season as runners-up.

Aberdeen slipped steadily, however, as international class players such as Buchan, Harper, Steve Murray and Willie Young found pastures new. An under-pressure Bonthrone tendered his resignation in October 1975.

The irrepressible Ally MacLeod didn't so much breathe fresh air around the stadium, as descend upon Pittodrie like a whirlwind. Ally instilled belief. Within a year the confidence stemming from the master of the rapier-quick chatter had the Dons in a League Cup final. Again the Reds tackled a formidable green and white obstacle.

Extrovert Ally had made telling alterations by handing the club captaincy to a youthful Willie Miller, by bringing Joe Harper back to the fold and by signing Stuart Kennedy and Dom Sullivan. Pittodrie, the players, the fans and some thought the city itself, were floating along on the crest of

98. Get your tickets here. Fans were snapping up six tickets at a time for the 1967 Scottish Cup semi final against Dundee United. 18,000 were sold within two hours.

MacLeod's wave of optimism.

Ally's faith was shown to be well founded when Dave Robb, another colourful character, rose from the Hampden bench to clinch the League Cup with a sensational extra-time winner (earlier, Drew Jarvie had cancelled Kenny Dalglish's penalty opener). Success, however, had its price for Aberdeen and the SFA whisked MacLeod away in May 1977 to overlord Scotland.

As Ally sprinted out, Billy McNeill - Celtic's Caesar - walked commandingly through the front door. Big Billy was also destined to have only a brief encounter with the Dons before, as sure as night turns to day, he took the road back to Paradise with Celtic.

McNeill laid solid foundations in the North-East corner before his departure and the club were later to benefit greatly from his foresight in securing Steve Archibald from his previous club, Clyde, and Gordon Strachan from Dundee, for virtual throwaway fees.

An instant favourite with the fans, McNeill's undeniable qualities as a leader came within a hairsbreadth of bringing the Championship and the Scottish Cup to Pittodrie. It didn't because Aberdeen simply and unexpectedly froze when confronted by a Rangers side which won by 2-1 to carry off the magic treble and leave a sad McNeill empty-handed.

Aberdeen were now left to seek their third manager in as many years. But not even the staunchest Red Army recruit could have guessed the riches that lay in store under Alex Ferguson.

99. Good luck kisses for Jim Storrie (*left*) and Jens Peterson from Pittodrie cleaners Mrs J Ryrie and Mrs A Gordon as the Dons leave to prepare for the 1967 Scottish Cup final.

100. Thumbs-up and smile, lads. But there were no happy faces on the return from Hampden after a 2-0 defeat.

101. Veteran keeper Ronnie Simpson booted this effort clear from the grounded Jens Peterson as Harry Melrose raced in. Looking on is Celtic captain Billy McNeill, who was to become the first British player to lift the European Cup just twenty-six days later.

102. Aberdeen's place in the Cup final gave them their European baptism. Here's the Dons first-ever European strike in the Cup-Winners' Cup against KR Reykjavik on 6 September 1967. Jim Storrie (*left*) watches a nineteenth minute Frank Munro header hit the net.

103. An international class save from Bobby Clark who once held the record of being the club's most capped player.

104. Cup-tie McKay gives his victory salute after scoring the only goal in the Scottish Cup semi final against Kilmarnock at Muirton in 1970.

105. Joe Harper created an all-time club record of 199 goals during two spells at Pittodrie. Signed from Morton for £40,000 in October 1969, he left for Everton three years later for £180,000. But in April 1976 Joe returned home to continue his net-bulging business, until a serious knee injury effectively ended his playing career.

Evening Express   Souvenir Edition
SIXTEEN PAGES OF PICTURES AND STORIES

SCOTTISH CUP 1970

The dandy Dons, Scottish Cup winners for season 1969-70. Top—Martin Buchan (captain) and Eddie Turnbull (manager). Left—Arthur Graham; Joe Harper and Derek McKay; Jim Forrest and Dave Robb. Right—Bobby Clark; George Murray and Henning Boel; Jim Hermiston and Tommy McMillan.

106. The *Evening Express* souvenir front page as the Dons made their way to Hampden.

The Don

Price 30p

The Champion's Matchday Companion

EUROPEAN CHAMPION CLUBS CUP

ABERDEEN v LIVERPOOL

ROUND TWO — FIRST LEG

Wednesday 22nd October

1980

EUROPEAN
CUP WINNERS' CUP

ABERDEEN FC
REAL MADRID CF

FINAL TIE OF MAY 11th 1983
GOTHENBURG • SWEDEN

SVENSKA FOTBOLLFÖRBUNDET

Pris: 5 Sek.

107 & 108. *above:* The precise penalty style which launched a thousand cheers. Joe Harper is spot on at Hampden. *below:* The ball is in the Celtic net and Derek McKay (not in picture) has struck.

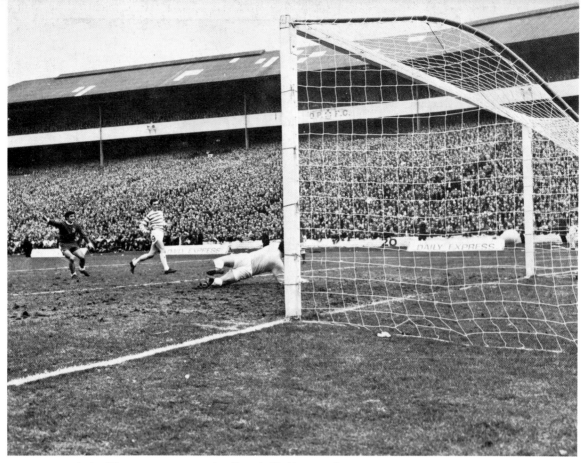

109. The cup goes north. Derek McKay made sure with this late clincher.

110. Cup-tie McKay wrote his name into Pittodrie folklore. Tommy Gemmell and Bertie Auld show their dejection as Derek celebrates.

111. Captain Martin Buchan turns to the Red Army to display the big prize.

112 & 113. *above:* Surely not a tear from iron-man manager Eddie Turnbull - but winning Scottish Cup finals can be an emotional affair. *right:* Skipper Martin Buchan and manager Eddie Turnbull emerge from Hampden with the Scottish Cup. Chief scout Bobby Calder follows on with the base.

114. The whole of Aberdeen wanted to see the Scottish Cup paraded down Union Street.

115. The Scottish Cup is back at Pittodrie. Manager Eddie Turnbull, who played for Hibs in the 1947 final defeat by the Dons, has the cup at his feet. *back row:* Teddy Scott (trainer), Tommy McMillan, Henning Boel, Jim Hermiston, Bobby Clark, Dave Robb, George Murray, Jimmy Bon'throne (coach). *front row:* Joe Harper, Derek McKay, Jim Forrest, manager Turnbull, Martin Buchan, George Buchan, Arthur Graham.

116. Kenny Dalglish slams an early penalty past a diving Bobby Clark to give the Celts a lead in the 1976 League Cup.

117 & 118. *above:* Drew Jarvie, who had pushed Dalglish for the penalty, turns to receive the acclaim after heading the Dons back on to level terms. *below:* Super sub Dave Robb slips the ball past Peter Latchford for a sensational extra-time winner.

119. The winners' platform at Hampden was to become a familiar footing for captain Willie Miller.
Here he collects his first trophy in 1976.

120. Drew Jarvie and Dave Robb keep hold of the silver.

121. Smokin' Joe Harper also prefers to try the Cup on
for size.

122 & 123. *above left:* The Bobby can't bear to look up as the Dons players allow their fans a closer look at the League Cup. For the PC is former Aberdeen captain Jim Hermiston, who had not long retired from the club. *above right:* For a man who had just scored the winner in a major Cup final, Dave Robb carries a surprisingly glum look as he sits on his own at the back of the bus.

124. The League Cup winners edge their way through the crowd in their open-topped bus.

125 & 126. *above left:* Ally's enthusiasm brought the League Cup to Pittodrie in 1976. Here the Dons' manager is joined in the back row by coach George Murray and secretary Ian Taggart. In front with the trophy are vice-chairman Chris Anderson, chairman Dick Donald and director Charles Forbes. *above right:* Steve Archibald signs for Aberdeen from Clyde for a bargain £20,000 in 1978. He was later transferred to Spurs for a record £880,000 and then on to Barcelona for over £1,000,000.

127. Despite a rousing reception even the Red Army can't cheer up a sombre manager Billy McNeill following a 2-1 Scottish Cup final defeat by Rangers in 1978.

128. Steve Ritchie's bizarre Cup final goal. The full-back didn't connect properly, but his up-and-under beat Peter McCloy.

129. We'll support you evermore . . . even in Cup final defeat. Aberdeen are back at Pittodrie without the Scottish Cup, but the fans still gave them a wonderful welcome home.

130. Young fan Gideon Rothnie captured a few famous autographs at Aberdeen's 75th birthday rally. Jackie Hather signs on, while looking on are Tony Harris, Archie Baird, Chris Anderson, Don Emery and Harry Yorston.

131. The changing face of Pittodrie - a £500,000 South Stand - is explained by vice-chairman Chris Anderson, as chairman Dick Donald looks on approvingly.

Dominance! 1978-1986

Aberdeen offered Alex Ferguson, a man ill-at-ease with St. Mirren's limited resources, the platform his talent and awareness deserved and demanded. The time was ripe for Aberdeen to ascend to previously unthought of heights, especially on foreign fields.

Before Ferguson made his presence felt at Pittodrie, Aberdeen had enjoyed only the occasional success. By the time Ferguson flitted to England the Dons were reaping in two major trophies a season. The fiery Ferguson usually got what he wanted . . . and for that the Red Army will be eternally grateful as he placed Aberdeen firmly on the European football map.

In eight silver-lined years of glory abroad and dominance at home, Ferguson collected the European Cup-Winners' Cup, the European Super Cup, four Scottish Cups, three Premier League Championships, the Skol Cup and a host of awards and accolades. There could have been so much more as Ferguson also had a string of seconds. Aberdeen supporters may never see the likes again.

When Manchester United moved in for Alex Ferguson OBE (Dons director and a manager under contract), it was inevitable he could not and would not refuse the challenge to raise the ailing Old Trafford giant from its slumber.

Yet Ferguson had to wait and display patience before breaking the Old Firm monopoly on the Premier League. Twice in 1979 he had contested the League Cup final and twice the Trophy stayed out of Ferguson's eager reach.

In the first final, against Rangers on 31 March 1979, controversy raged when two late goals gave the Cup to Rangers after Doug Rougvie had been sensationally red-carded for an alleged offence involving Derek Johnstone. To this day Rougvie's guilt remains a mystery.

The second final was against Dundee United, the other half of the emerging New Firm who should have been beaten on the trip to Hampden in December. But United escaped to fight another day after a goalless draw. The replay at Dens Park brought a new initiative from the team from just across the road and a troubled Aberdeen were sunk 3-0 on a dreary, rain-soaked night.

What a contrast when Ferguson's champions-designate ventured with their Red Army in tow to Easter Road on 3 May 1980. From the Press Box I brought an end to Ferguson's title tensions when I signalled that nearest challengers Celtic had finished 0-0 at Paisley and the five goals hammered into the Hibs net were enough to make history.

Champions at last! And Ferguson spontaneously erupted into a jig-of-joy and congratulated each and every player and saluted the fans for their heart-felt support. Celebrations, if not the accompanying dance, were to become commonplace. The Scottish Cup, like the title, had been a long time in making its

132. Alex Ferguson steps inside Pittodrie for the first time as manager in the summer of 1978. But not even he could have envisaged the glories that lay ahead during his eight-year reign.

way to the North-East. Ferguson altered that statistic - and how!

Aberdeen's Union Street was to be awash with jubilant Dons fans four times in five years as the open-topped bus carried the Cup to its second home at Pittodrie. In 1982, 1983 and again in 1984 the Red Army clocked up overtime at Hampden as the Dons waited until extra time before fitting the Cup out in red-and-white ribbons.

Rangers were eventually swamped by a relentless red tide in that opening final, while the following year Eric Black's trademark - a black beauty of a header - kept the Cup. Aberdeen had fielded their Gothenburg heroes, but perfectionist Ferguson publicly lambasted his winners for a tired display. Second thoughts on a remarkable achievement later brought an apology.

The ninety-ninth Cup final with Celtic at the other end of Hampden was another crammed with incident, especially when Paul McStay equalised after Roy Aitken had been ordered off. Mark McGhee, in his last game before signing for Hamburg, supplied the winning touch of class.

Ferguson, much to his annoyance, missed out on the hundredth final when Dundee United won a heated semi final replay. But the Dons bounced back the next year. It was a cut-and-dried affair against a demoralised Hearts who had just suffered the agony of having the title swiped from them on the last League day. Two-goal John Hewitt and Billy Stark showed no sympathy or mercy.

A few months earlier Hearts' capital rivals Hibs had gone a similar way as Ferguson captured the Skol Cup/League Cup. Two from Black, and another customary counter from Stark, completed Aberdeen's Sunday stroll.

Aberdeen had become fierce and renowned Cup fighters, but Ferguson also had loving eyes for the Championship. In season 1983-84 the Dons were out in front after only a handful of matches. They never looked back. Next term's report was even better as Ferguson took the lead on the opening day . . . and stayed there. Aberdeen even broke their total points record for the Premier League with fifty-nine. And for good measure their eighty-nine goals set a postwar record for Pittodrie.

Ferguson had the imagination and the right players to fulfil his ideas. He also had the tactical sharpness of the tireless Archie Knox at his side. Knox followed Pat Stanton and Willie Garner as Ferguson's assistant manager. After a couple of years in charge of Dundee, football circles were astounded in 1986 when Knox was named as Aberdeen's co-manager, a position then unique in Scotland. Knox also took the route to Manchester with Ferguson that same year.

The Aberdeen chairman and his directors had to recover from the trauma of the double departure to select a manager to follow the Midas men. The answer lay in England. Ian Porterfield was their surprise selection.

133. Perhaps Alex Ferguson is seeking Divine intervention. Anyway, his prayers were answered as Aberdeen beat Celtic 1-0 in this 1983 match.

134. Joint managers Archie Knox and Alex Ferguson with their 1986 haul of silver in the boardroom.

135. Steve Archibald's header soars into the Hibs net as the Dons hit five for the 1980 title.

136. Alex McLeish is almost buried under a sea of bodies as the Red Army celebrate at Easter Road.

137. Alex Ferguson's jig-of-joy stopped when he acclaimed the fans.

138. Champagne and soapy water - what a mix. But the Dons were Champions.

139. Alex Ferguson's first victory parade down Union Street. Many more were to follow.

140. The first Premier flag is swept around Pittodrie. Eric Black (*right*) had the honour that day, but in the not-too-distant future he was to blossom into the club's scoring kingpin.

XX & XXI. We will follow on. The Red Army troop behind the victors and their spoils past the Town House.

XXII. We won the Cup. 1986 final scorers John Hewitt
and Billy Stark have their hands full. Hewitt also won
the Man-of-the-Match award.

XXIII. 1986 Scottish Cup Final.

141. Aberdeen bringing the Championship Trophy home.

142. Alastair Guthrie hands over two special *Evening Express* commemorative plaques to Alex Ferguson.

143. Gordon Strachan starts the Championship ball rolling in
1983-84 with the opening goal of the season,
a penalty against Dundee.

144. John Hewitt acrobatically scores against Dundee United in 1985 - and the Dons were well on the way to retaining their crown.

145. The title clincher. And scorer Willie Miller couldn't have written a better script.

146. Bring out the bubbly. We're Champions again.

147. Frank McDougall heading the first of a hat-trick past Rangers' Nicky Walker. The keeper was beaten five times that January afternoon in 1985. Fabulous Frank went on to establish a new club Premier League record with twenty-two goals.

CUT ABOVE

148 & 149. *left:* A cut above, right enough. Chairman Dick Donald, Scottish League secretary Jim Farry, director Ian Donald, vice-chairman Chris Anderson and secretary Ian Taggart admire a new flag. *above:* More sweeping developments at Pittodrie in 1985 as the Paddock is pulled down to make way for a new enclosure exclusively reserved for Dons fans.

150. Pittodrie is developing all the time. This 1984 aerial shot captures the new South Stand (*top*). Work was soon to progress at the Paddock and Beach End.

152. *above:* Alex McLeish is in there somewhere as he is mobbed by team-mates after his brilliantly-executed equaliser.

151. 1982 gave skipper Willie Miller his hat-trick of domestic medals and many more were to follow.

153. *below:* Alex Ferguson imparts a few words of wisdom to Gordon Strachan at the end of full-time. Strachan went on to score in extra-time.

154. So did Mark McGhee.

155. And Neale Cooper was in splendid isolation to blast in a fourth from point blank range.

156. The Red Army had high hopes for the 1982 Scottish Cup final.

157. Willie Miller lets the Red Army see the Scottish Cup. He had to turn around to collect his winner's medal.

158. Archie Knox and Alex Ferguson show off trophy which was to have Pittodrie as its second home.

159, 160 & 161. *above:* Once more in 1983 Alex Ferguson had to tell his troops exactly what was required in extra time. *right:* That's my boy. Trainer Teddy Scott congratulates a chuffed Eric Black. *below:* The pep talk brought dividends again as Eric Black scored near the end of extra-time.

162. John McMaster and Jim Leighton keep a grip on the Cup. Lining up behind the pair are Gordon Strachan, Andy Watson, Mark McGhee, Doug Rougvie, Neil Simpson, Peter Weir, Alex McLeish, Neale Cooper, Willie Miller, Eric Black, John Hewitt.

163. An agile Eric Black has the ball in the Celtic net early on in a dramatic 1984 Scottish Cup final.

164. The irresistible force meets the immovable object. Strong men Doug Rougvie and Roy Aitken clash at Hampden.

165. Mark McGhee's last-ever kick of the ball for Aberdeen - the extra-time Scottish Cup winner. The striker would soon be on his way to Hamburg for £280,000.

166. Flashpoint. Roy Aitken (*right*) exchanges words with Gordon Strachan before the Celt was red-carded for a body-check on Mark McGhee, who is receiving treatment.

XXIV. On the mark at Hampden as Mark McGhee
punishes Celtic in the Scottish Cup final.

XXV. Alex Ferguson bellows out his orders for victory
at Hampden.

XXVI. The Red Army celebrates.

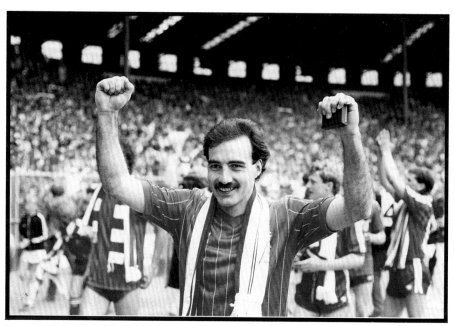

XXVII. Willie Miller clutches another winner's medal as he salutes
the Red Army's support.

XXVIII. These ladies in red are singing in the rain as they await
the arrival of the successful Dons.

XXIX, The Dons undertake another victory parade.

XXX. The Cup arrives at Pittodrie.

XXXI. Alex Ferguson obliges with an autograph on a ball while Alex McLeish sips the last of the champagne.

XXXII. Smiles from Alex Ferguson.

167. That's the hat-trick. The Dons bench begin the celebrations.

168. John Hewitt's happy Hampden day in the 1986 Scottish Cup final as he cracks in the opening goal.

169. Billy Stark completes the misery for Hearts with a characteristic diving header.

170. Two-goal John Hewitt gets into focus, but Billy Stark was still receiving touch-line congratulations. At the back are Jim Leighton, Jim Bett, Peter Weir, John Hewitt. In front are Neale Cooper, Stewart McKimmie, Frank McDougall, Willie Miller, Alex McLeish, Tommy McQueen, Joe Miller and John McMaster.

171. Billy Stark now has a hand on the Cup as Alex Ferguson and his Dons chuckle at a Neale Cooper joke.

172. Here we are again as Alex Ferguson shows the Red Army the Scottish Cup from the balcony at the Town House.

173 & 174. *above:* 1979 was a bad Cup year. In March Duncan Davidson gave the Dons the lead against Rangers in the League Cup final. But after Doug Rougvie's controversial ordering-off the Light Blues stormed back with two goals. The Dons show their reaction to Colin Jackson's cup winner. *below:* And in December the Dons lost a Dens Park replay by 3-0 to Dundee United after a goalless League Cup final at Hampden. The expressions on the faces of Steve Archibald, Willie Miller and Bobby Clark say it all, although they sportingly applaud United's first major triumph.

175. Eric Black puts on his Sunday best to head in the first of his two goals in Aberdeen's easy 3-0 League Cup final win over Hibs in 1985.

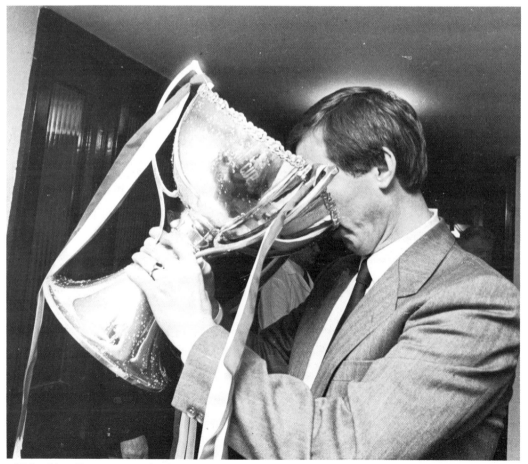

176. Alex Ferguson waited seven years before landing the elusive League Cup, so he has an extra mouthful of champagne.

Into Europe

177. Aberdeen's education was furthered by Liverpool in their 1980 European Cup encounters. Willie Miller leads out his Dons, but Liverpool had the experience of Kenny Dalglish and Graeme Souness to call on.

178. Swiss side Sion were the first to roll on the way to the European Cup-Winners' Cup at Gothenburg and Mark McGhee scored the sixth of Aberdeen's magnificent seven at Pittodrie.

179. Then came Dinamo Tirana from Albania, who were knocked out by this cool John Hewitt strike.

180. Next to go were Lech Poznan, who lost at Pittodrie and again in Poland. They had no answer to the spring-heeled Eric Black.

181 & 182. *above:* The hidden Alex McLeish made it 2-2 with this header which just eluded Bayern keeper Muller. *below:* And Bayern were bamboozled when super sub John Hewitt poked the winner through Muller's legs.

183. Waterschei were no semi final match for the Dons at Pittodrie. Neil Simpson jumps on Eric Black's back after the young attacker had scored the first of five after only eighty seconds.

184. Then it was Neil Simpson's turn to score a quick second goal to further bemuse the Belgians.

185. The 1984 European Super Cup. The Dons had victory in their pockets after a grounded Neil Simpson opened the scoring in the forty-seventh minute against European Cup holders SV Hamburg.

186. And Mark McGhee made certain of this unique victory by slotting in a second goal in the sixty-fourth minute.

XXXIII. Players and wives gather round the Scottish Cup at a
private club party.

XXXIV & XXXV. Gentle giant Doug Rougvie shows off the Cup-Winners' Cup to the fans.

187. The best in Europe. That was Aberdeen's official designation after beating Hamburg.
Willie Miller displays the Super Cup plaque. *back row:* Doug Bell, Jim Leighton, John Hewitt,
Alex McLeish, Gordon Strachan, Neil Simpson, Peter Weir, Stewart McKimmie.
front row: Willie Miller, John McMaster, Mark McGhee, Eric Black.

More to Follow

Ian Porterfield openly acknowledged that he had a hard act to follow when introductions were made in the Pittodrie boardroom in November 1986. His words were to be prophetic, as his stay was only a relatively brief eighteen months. Porterfield's name hadn't been mentioned when the fans debated a successor to Alex Ferguson and the tall, relaxed Fifer was definitely the dark horse.

His first task was to consolidate Aberdeen's position and to guarantee that European football, so vital to the Dons, would continue at Pittodrie. Both targets were achieved, but Porterfield's pack suffered from being paired with Celtic at the opening Scottish Cup hurdle. Still, it took three games before the Celts slipped through.

The man, forever remembered as the midfielder who upset all the odds by scoring the winner for underdogs Sunderland in the 1973 FA Cup final against a seemingly invincible Leeds, then made his first serious signing move by paying £350,000 to Luton for Welsh international midfield player Peter Nicholas.

Porterfield had to restructure his side following the loss of free scoring Billy Stark, who wanted to leave, and master marksman Frank McDougall, who was cruelly forced out of the game with back problems.

Porterfield had been unceremoniously dismissed by Sheffield United eight months before Aberdeen sent out their call . . . despite leading the club out of the wilderness of the Fourth Division and into a promotion-chasing position in the Second Division. He knew all about the highs and lows in football. And he had the character to fight, having battled back to fitness within two months following a near-fatal car crash.

But that first piece of silver remained elusive, just as it had been for Ferguson. Porterfield was denied the break he wanted in a drama-packed 1987 Skol Cup final. Big-spending Rangers were down by 3-2 to the Dons as they entered the closing minutes of the best contest of the season. But fact, as Porterfield was to find out, can be stranger than fiction.

Rangers revived to equalise and, after an eventless extra-time, won the first penalty kick shoot-out ever to decide a major Cup final at Hampden. Peter Nicholas had sleepless nights for weeks after his spot miss paved the way for Iain Durrant's decider.

Porterfield's side were solid enough at the back. But an infection of flair was required - so who

188. The Scottish Cup was still in the boardroom when vice-chairman Ian Donald and chairman Dick Donald introduced new manager Ian Porterfield to the assembled Press in November 1986.

better than Charlie Nicholas, the former Celtic darling who was enduring a trying period of exile in England with Arsenal? As 1987 made way for 1988 Porterfield sent a club record of £400,000 on its way to the Gunners for the skilled striker with the champagne style.

And it was Charlie, an instant hit with the Red Army, who almost took the Dons into the 1988 Scottish Cup final. Those troublesome Cup competitors, Dundee United, having been reduced to ten men, found themselves a goal behind in a Dens Park semi final replay when Charlie conjured up a vintage goal.

But the fightback and another game gave victory to the Tannadice men, leaving Porterfield deliberating on what should have been. His soul-searching lasted only days after the season closed, as Porterfield tendered his resignation to the Pittodrie board on 16 May 1988 "for family reasons".

Just before Porterfield departed, World Cup keeper Jim Leighton brought an end to a distinguished era by moving to Manchester United for £750,000 under freedom of contract. But in typical fashion the international player created a club record of thirty-five shut-outs in fifty-nine games before announcing his decision to go after more than a decade's sterling service.

Alex Smith had been invited to join the Pittodrie coaching staff shortly before Porterfield cleared out his desk and only weeks after being rejected by St. Mirren, despite his Scottish Cup success the previous year.

It was quiet man Smith who was to take over the helm after Aberdeen's fifteen managerless days. And for the second time in their history the Dons named a co-manager, this time former Pittodrie striker and Dundee boss, Jocky Scott. To complete the new-look management team another of the Red Army's former favourite players, Drew Jarvie, also took the road from Dens back to Pittodrie. Scott and Jarvie had previously tasted success with the Dons and now Aberdeen's top trio of coaches were set to renew their search for silver.

189. First day at the office . . . and new boss Ian Porterfield gets to know his first-team squad. *back row:* Jim Leighton, Billy Stark, Alex McLeish, Willie Miller, Paul Wright, Davie Dodds, Stewart McKimmie, Dave Robertson, Brian Mitchell, Jim Bett. *front row:* Bobby Connor, the manager, Joe Miller, John Hewitt, Peter Weir, John McMaster.

190. Turning on the heat at Pittodrie. Around twenty-six miles of pipe for the undersoil heating system are buried below the pitch in 1987.

191. Peter Nicholas had Ian Porterfield and Ian Donald grinning after the Welsh international moved north from Luton for £350,000 in August 1987.

192. Training sessions in Aberdeen can be pretty wind-battered, chilly occasions. Neither trainer Teddy Scott nor manager Ian Porterfield seem to know which direction the wind is coming from. But they certainly know where it is going!

193. Nicholas, however, was a picture of total dejection in season 1987-88 after a miss in a penalty shoot-out in the Skol Cup final against Rangers at Hampden. The Light Blues collected the Cup.

194 & 195. *above:* Cheery Charlie Nicholas brought smiles to the faces of vice-chairman Ian Donald and chairman Dick Donald in the boardroom following his club record £400,000 transfer from Arsenal in January 1988. *below:* Manager Ian Porterfield helps Charlie Nicholas try out his new colours.

196. Aberdeen's strike force of Charlie Nicholas and Davie Dodds.

197. The main door at Pittodrie has been thrown open to Drew Jarvie, Alex Smith and Jocky Scott, who immediately show their allegiance to the Dons.

198. Aberdeen's longest serving player just happens to be the most capped in the club's history - Willie Miller, of course. Willie signed a new contract in the summer of 1988 and will complete his playing career at Pittodrie.

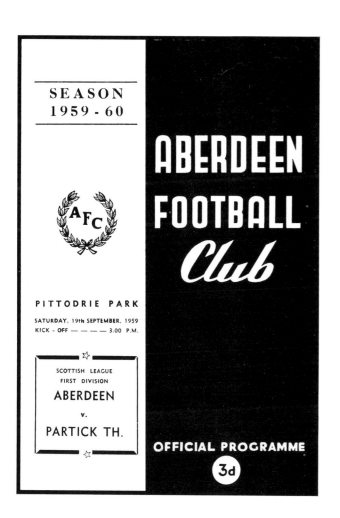

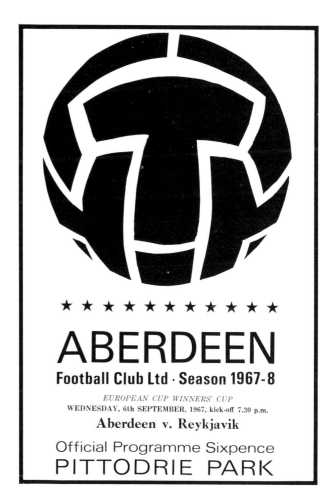

199, 200 & 201. *top left:* Official programme for a League game against Partick Thistle. The Dons won 5-2 with Hughie Baird and Jim Clunie scoring two apiece and Billy Little scoring one. *top right:* Aberdeen's first venture into the European Cup-winners' Cup 6 September 1967. The game was played before a crowd of 14,000 and Aberdeen built up a respectable four goal lead by half-time. In the second half the Dons destroyed Reykjavik with a further six goals. *left:* The UEFA Cup. Having disposed of Celta Vigo in Round One, the Dons went on to meet Juventus eventually losing 1-3 on aggregate.

ABERDEEN v. BORUSSIA MUNCHENGLADBACH

7.30 | **M**ATCH-DAY **M**AGAZINE | **5p**

U.E.F.A. CUP — FIRST ROUND (FIRST LEG)

SCOTTISH LEAGUE CUP Wednesday August 22 1973.

ABERDEEN v DUNDEE UNITED

WILLIE MILLER, at 18 years, the youngest member of the Aberdeen team in the last two matches.

ABERDEEN FC
(FOUNDED 1903)
PITTODRIE STADIUM
ABERDEEN AB2 1QH
TELEPHONE: 21428

Chairman:
R.M. DONALD
Vice-Chairman:
C. ANDERSON
Directors:
C.B. FORBES
(Past Chairman)
R.E. SPAIN
Manager:
J. BONTHRONE
Secretary:
M.D. RANKIN

Scottish League champions 1954-55.
Runners-up 1910-11, 1936-37, 1955-56, 1970-71, 1971-72.
Scottish Cup winners, 1947, 1970.
Finalists 1937, 1953, 1954, 1959, 1967.
Scottish League Cup winners 1945-46, 1955-56.
Finalists 1946-47.
Dryborough Cup winners 1971.

5p

Dons		UNITED
Bobby CLARK	1	Hamish McALPINE
Billy WILLIAMSON	2	Andy ROLLAND
Jim HERMISTON	3	Jim CAMERON
Eddie THOMSON	4	Jackie COPLAND
Willie YOUNG	5	Doug SMITH
Willie MILLER	6	Walter SMITH
Joe SMITH	7	Kenny CAMERON
Arthur GRAHAM	8	Duncan McLEOD
Ian TAYLOR	9	Graeme PAYNE
Drew JARVIE	10	Jim HENRY
Ian PURDIE	11	Tommy TRAYNOR
SUBS		

MATCH OFFICIALS:
Referee: R.H. DAVIDSON (Airdrie)
Linesmen: I.A. MUNRO (Linlithgow)
J.F. KERON (Coupar Angus)

ABERDEEN

Referee: C. LO BELLOE (Italy)

1 BOBBY CLARK 2 IAN HAIR 3 JIM HERMISTON
4 EDDIE THOMSON 5 WILLIE YOUNG 6 WILLIE MILLER
7 ALEX WILLOUGHBY 8 DAVE ROBB 9 ARTHUR GRAHAM

SUBSTITUTES
....

10 DREW JARVIE 11 BERTIE MILLER

TOTTENHAM

1	Pat JENNINGS	6	Philip BEAL
2	Ray EVANS	7	Alan GILZEAN
3	Cyril KNOWLES	8	Steve PERRYMAN
4	John PRATT	9	Martin CHIVERS
5	Mike ENGLAND	10	Martin PETERS
		11	Ralph COATES

SUBSTITUTES
....

UEFA CUP SECOND ROUND FIRST LEG

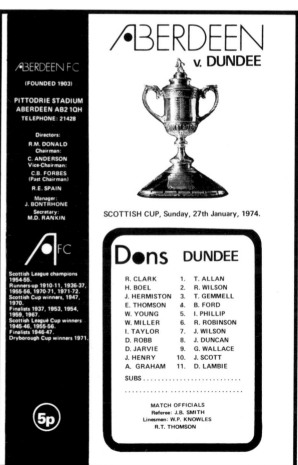

ABERDEEN v. DUNDEE

ABERDEEN FC
(FOUNDED 1903)
PITTODRIE STADIUM
ABERDEEN AB2 1QH
TELEPHONE: 21428

Directors:
R.M. DONALD
Chairman:
C. ANDERSON
Vice-Chairman:
C.B. FORBES
(Past Chairman)
R.E. SPAIN
Manager:
J. BONTRHONE
Secretary:
M.D. RANKIN

Scottish League champions 1954-55.
Runners-up 1910-11, 1936-37, 1955-56, 1970-71, 1971-72.
Scottish Cup winners, 1947, 1970.
Finalists 1937, 1953, 1954, 1959, 1967.
Scottish League Cup winners 1945-46, 1955-56.
Finalists 1946-47.
Dryborough Cup winners 1971.

SCOTTISH CUP, Sunday, 27th January, 1974.

5p

Dons		DUNDEE
R. CLARK	1.	T. ALLAN
H. BOEL	2.	R. WILSON
J. HERMISTON	3.	T. GEMMELL
E. THOMSON	4.	B. FORD
W. YOUNG	5.	I. PHILLIP
W. MILLER	6.	R. ROBINSON
I. TAYLOR	7.	J. WILSON
D. ROBB	8.	J. DUNCAN
D. JARVIE	9.	G. WALLACE
J. HENRY	10.	J. SCOTT
A. GRAHAM	11.	D. LAMBIE
SUBS		

MATCH OFFICIALS
Referee: J.B. SMITH
Linesmen: W.P. KNOWLES
R.T. THOMSON

202-205. More games to remember.

EP der Landesmeister

Europapokal der Landesmeister

1. Runde 1984/85 Rückspiel

Mittwoch,
3. Oktober 1984
17 Uhr

Friedrich-Ludwig-
Jahn-Sportpark

Programm: 16 S.   0,50 M

BFC DYNAMO

FC ABERDEEN

EUROPACUP DER LANDESMEISTER

AUSTRIA MEMPHIS : F.C. ABERDEEN

1. Oktober 1980, Wiener Stadion

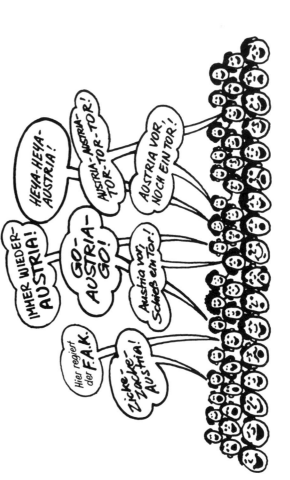

DM 1,–

Bayern
ZIN

Club- und Stadionzeitschrift
des F.C. Bayern München e.V.
Europapokal   2. März 198_

Viertelfinale

Bayern München
FC Aberdeen

Daten, Fakten, Zahlen
Alles über
den FC Aberdeen

Facts and Figures

Premier Division Champions:	1979-80, 1983-84, 1984-85
Division One Champions:	1954-55
Scottish Cup Winners:	1947, 1970, 1982, 1983, 1984, 1986
Scottish League Cup Winners:	1955-56, 1976-77, 1985-86
Scottish Southern League Cup:	1945-46
European Cup-Winners' Cup winners:	1983
European Super Cup:	1983

Record Scottish Cup victory:	13-0 v Peterhead, 3rd Round, 9 February 1923.
Record League Cup win:	9-0 v Queen of the South, Qualifying Section, 13 September 1947; 9-0 v Raith Rovers, 2nd Round !st Leg, 24 August 1983.
Record League win:	10-0 v Raith Rovers, 13 October 1962.
Record Away win:	7-1 v Airdrie, 28 September 1963.
Record Home defeat:	0-5 v Hearts, 8 April 1950; v Rangers, 24 October 1959; v Partick Thistle, 28 December 1963.
Record Away defeat:	0-8 v Celtic, 30 January 1965.
Record attendance:	45,061 v Hearts, Scottish Cup 4th Round, 13 March 1954.
Record Away attendance:	63,000 v Celtic, 12 December 1970.
Record League Cup attendance:	82,684 v Rangers, Final at Hampden, 5 April 1947.
Record Scottish Cup attendance:	146,433 v Celtic, Final, 24 April 1937.

Most consecutive appearances:	Ally Shewan (197).
Most appearances:	Willie Miller
Most goals scored in one game:	Alex Merrie (6); Paddy Moore (6).
Most goals scored in one season:	Benny Yorston (38).

209.   Aberdeen's Mo. 1 fan ... the Green Final's Wee Alickie. Saturday nights wouldn't be the same without Wee Alickie's wit.

210. Hungarian Zolton Varga - some would argue the most naturally gifted player to wear a Don's strip - knew exactly what he was doing on the pitch. But Dane Henning Boel was required to act as interpreter for manager Jimmy Bonthrone on Varga's arrival in 1972.

Acknowledgements

My sincere thanks go to several people who helped make this pictorial history possible, none more so than the many photographers and printers, past and present, of *Aberdeen Journals*; to *Aberdeen Journals* librarian Tom Forsyth and his staff for limitless patience; to Aberdeen FC secretary Ian Taggart for helping to sift through the charred club photographs salvaged from that 1971 blaze at Pittodrie; to the Aberdeen FC board of directors for their willingness and guidance; to Moyra, Laurie, Fraser, Greer and to many friends and colleagues for their support.

For the Red Army.